THE HAND

OF

GOD

A Story of Divine Healing

Nokuzola Mangcotywa

Published By

Peaches

Publications

Published in London by Peaches Publications, 2023.

www.peachespublications.co.uk

The moral right of the author has been asserted.

All rights reserved. No part of this book may be reproduced, stored in a retrieval system, or transmitted in any form or by any means, electronic, mechanical, photocopying, recording, public performances or otherwise, without written permission of Nokuzola Mangcotywa, except for brief quotations embodied in critical articles or reviews. The book is for personal use only; commercial use is prohibited unless written permission and a licence are obtained from the author Nokuzola Mangcotywa.

The right of Nokuzola Mangcotywa to be identified as the author of this work has been asserted in accordance with sections 77 and 78 of the copyright Designs and Patents Act 1988.

Text Copyright © 2023 by Nokuzola Mangcotywa

British Library Cataloguing in Publication Data: A catalogue record for this book is available from the British Library.

ISBN: 9798368358062

Book cover design: Peaches Publications

Editor: Linda Green

Typesetter: Linda Green and Winsome Duncan

Proofreader: Virginia Rounding

Table of Contents

Dedication 1
Acknowledgements 2
Foreword 9
Introduction 15
What Went Wrong 17
Where It All Started 23
How God Revealed Himself 34
Divine Support / Truthvine Family Church Support 49
The Children 58
Sisterhood and Family 70
Being Used Amidst Adversity 80
Divine Helpers 87
God Sustained Me Throughout the Journey 101
The Father Heart of God 109
About the Author 117
Useful Agency 120
References 121

Dedication

I would like to dedicate this book to my Lord and Saviour, who has been with me throughout this experience. He has provided help when I needed it in tangible and practical ways. He has lifted me up when I was down, and not only that, He has helped me to consider others even in my time of need.

I have grown to love my LORD through this experience, and I have grown in my trust in Him.

I also want to dedicate this book to my readers. May you find hope in this book that builds your love for God, and may it help you to trust Him in all situations, because He is an ever-present help in times of trouble.

Acknowledgements

I want to thank God for inspiring me to write about my experiences so that others can be blessed by what He has done for me. I do not have adequate words to thank you, Lord, for your support, provision, and placing the right people along my path at the right times. If I did not know it before, I know it now: in you, Lord, I live and move and have my being (Acts 17:28).

Gratitude to my late grandparents, Makhaya and Dora Mangcotywa, whom I grew up with. They sowed the seed of faith, taking me to church regularly from a young age. They taught me to love the Lord, and that love has taken me through my recovery.

My siblings, Tembisa, Siphokazi, Mzwandile, and Dumani, for your love, support, and faith in me. I love you all dearly.

Jongizizwe Ntilashe, my best friend, supported me when I visited South Africa following the Monster Attack. You showed genuine love and concern, demonstrated in your actions and how you treated me. You made me feel valued and loved. Thank you.

My extended family. I love you also. Thank you for your encouragement, love and support. You are all that honour, loyalty, and family should look like.

Reverend Betty King, thank you for supporting me as a minister of Christ and as a church mother. You missed nothing. You organised people to support me spiritually, physically, and emotionally. I do not have adequate words to thank you. Like a faithful mother, you surrounded me with persons who have become family to me, not distant but close family. You ensured I did not feel alone, or neglected, or forgotten. As if that was not enough, you encouraged me to write my story, and in doing so, I could see the goodness of my God. I thank God for your life and honour you and your ministry.

The Truthvine community have been wonderful. Like a good vine, you provided me with sustenance and support. You adopted me, loved me and cared for me. Thank you!

I want to thank my many friends from the body of Christ who supported me along the way. Pastor Raymond Thorne, Pastor Mawuli Doe, Prophet Levi Van Buuren and his wife Aimee, and Pastor Thabisa Xhentsa.

Kemi Bamgbose, you are a jewel that gleams in this world. This book would not have existed if it was not for you. You had a vision for me and this book and encouraged me to put my experiences down. Somehow you connected with something the Lord had already put in my heart. You confirmed that I should write, and because of that, I embarked on writing this book. God bless you. Ancilla Davids-Saba - you have been more than a neighbour to me, your family became mine. Thank you for your love and kindness.

To the South African diaspora, I have seen the spirit of "ubuntu" in you, and you have demonstrated to me that no man is an island. You made me feel loved.

My friends in South Africa: Nosisi Lufuso, Mpumi Maseko, Nolita

Nkomana, Pearl Nqwemesha, Patiswa Kula and Nolita Peter. You did not make distance a problem. You kept near with your calls and texts, and you encouraged me through the rough times. You saw in me something I did not even think I had. You valued me and helped me feel strong again despite my weakness. Thank you so much.

My local friends, how can I thank you all? You were there for me even when I wanted to give up. You did not allow me to wallow. You took the rough with the smooth and showed me how to make lemon juice from what I saw as lemons. God bless you all.

Sandra Surrey, thank you so much for your friendship, support and encouragement through this experience, which was always timely. Thank you for writing the Foreword for this book. I cannot fully express in words my gratitude to you.

Thank you, Linda Green, for scribing and editing my book. You have a calm, professional disposition that made me feel encouraged. You understood my heart and were able to write my feelings in words. Blessings!

The Peaches Publications Team, especially Winsome, have encouraged me and ensured that I progressed my work. You believed in me as an author, and you believed that I have a story to tell, a message for the world. Your spirit of excellence has pushed me to ensure that I complete the work so the world can be blessed. Thank you!

Scripture quotations marked (NKJV) are taken from the New King James Version. Copyright © 1982 by

Thomas Nelson, Inc. Used by permission. All rights reserved.

Foreword

My formative years did not give me a picture of a good father. The fact was, I did not have a father figure. No affirmation. The words were mainly, "*God will punish you if you do or don't do this or that. The reason you're sick is because of your disobedience.*" How many of you can identify with these words? Since then, there has been a paradigm shift in my theology, thanks to the revelations through Bill Johnson's *God is Good* and Danny Silk's Unpunishable.

I think it was in 2015, whilst I was at a healing retreat in Farnham, that I heard the very powerful musical voice of a South African singer. I didn't know then, as I approached her and quietly asked whether she was from South Africa, that Zola and I would become friends. Nelson Mandela's *Long Walk To Freedom* captured my heart, and I fell in love with the resilience and feisty personalities of the South African people. There were times when I wished I was from one of their tribes.

This book you are about to read and meditate on is Zola's personal "long walk" with God, the Healer. She appropriates what Jesus did 2,000 years ago – "by His stripes we are healed" (Isaiah 53:5). This includes physical, emotional, and psychological healing. You will laugh, cry and question God, but keep reading until the end. It is about a loving God who "permitted" an illness, but holds Zola's hand through the provisions and prayers of medical professionals and His faithful believers.

My friend had called me to pray with her on her arrival at Lewisham Hospital. On my first and subsequent visits, we worshipped and took communion with Jesus. I danced before the Lord for Zola and me in her "private" room. You see, I believed in a Good God and that the taking of communion and dancing were weapons of warfare.

When Zola asked me to proofread the first draft, I felt so honoured that I immediately purchased a laptop and took a couple of train journeys to Hastings. I needed uninterrupted time to meet the deadline. However, my assignment was to "edit". I took the draft everywhere. One day, while visiting an elderly friend (now with the Lord) in Mayday University Hospital, a young female patient came out needing a cigarette. She started sharing with me her many conditions and experiences. I got the impression from the Holy Spirit that this was a divine appointment to share what God was doing for and with Zola. I quickly texted her and got her permission to share from the book. I listened to the young lady and asked whether I could share something I was reading. She agreed. She listened as I read. I finished reading just as her cigarette died. She thanked me and returned inside to her ward with the goodness of God chasing after her. I must mention that this was the second time I had shared from the draft.

I have been walking with my sissy through her journey of recovery. I have enjoyed serving her in the small ways God has enabled me to. I am a walker, but in October 2019, I was led to purchase a car. I sensed God wanted me to buy one of beauty and not practicality. I recalled the summer of 2021; Zola was desperate to get out. So, we arranged an outing to the Horniman Museum, Forest Hill. Imagine delight of both of us! I was driving at 5mph in our Alfa Remo Mito, royal blue, on the grounds, with indicators flashing, as folks stepped aside and looked on. The "Royal Daughters" had been made to look regal by the Father's provision. We both had uncontrollable joy, knowing the goodness of the Father.

The Hand of God is Zola's journey through her ongoing story of healing and restoration. Her story tells of a loving, caring Father, who uses His children to support, encourage and lift up His saints when times are hard, and struggles are real. He brings light to those who may feel trapped in a dark tunnel of despair when they are oppressed by the evil one.

God has demonstrated in Zola's story that He is always near, always provides, and always protects His children.

As you read, be blessed!

Sandra Surrey

Introduction

I have always been interested in words from a young age. My late grandfather would ask me to read for him, and he encouraged my expressions as I read. I enjoyed morphing into different characters and interjecting feelings in my storytelling. Granddad could read but loved to encourage me.

It is no wonder that I felt compelled to write my story. I know how powerful and encouraging it can be for others who may be going through a similar experience or who may be supporting someone post-stroke or some other life-changing trauma. I hope my story will take you through the dark and difficult days and show you that there is light at the end of the tunnel.

Most of all, I want the reader to know that strength comes from the Lord, the maker of heaven and earth. You can lean on Him; He will be there with you even when you do not think He is.

> I will lift up my eyes to the hills –
> From whence comes my help? My help *comes* from the Lord, Who made heaven and earth. Psalm 121:1, 2.

As you read, be encouraged and be blessed!

Zola Mangcotywa

What Went Wrong

> **Beloved, I pray that you may prosper in all things and be in health, just as your soul prospers.**
> **3 John 1:2 (NKJV)**

20 January 2020 was just an ordinary morning, like any other. I woke up and praised the Lord and said my favourite scripture – *"This is the day the LORD has made; We will rejoice and be glad in it"* (Psalm 118:24). So, I started my day the usual way. Fortunately, it was a Monday morning, and I was still fired up from the previous service on Sunday. I woke up and was full of joy. There was nothing strange or unusual as I was working

from home. Praise God! I started to do my work, and as I was working, I had this song playing in mind which was written by Zenzo Matoga and Philip Nathan Thompson, and sung by Phil Thompson.

You Lord, You are worthy
And no one can worship You for me
For all the things You've done for me
And no one can worship You for me

Here's my worship
All of my worship
Receive my worship
All of my worship
Here's my worship
All of my worship
Receive my worship
All of my worship.

I was working and humming and singing to myself. As they say in my language, "no day ends without news". That day was to end with some news that was not great for me.

So around early afternoon, 2.00 p.m., I was sitting on the sofa and suddenly, out of the blue, I felt this kind of sensation in my head. It felt like something had popped into my head. But before we continue, I would like to go back a bit.

The diagnosis

In 2015 I had these blinding headaches, and after some time, I decided that I should see the doctor because this was bothering me. I was diagnosed with high blood pressure. At that point, I was 48. I was advised to manage my blood pressure and given medication. However, I sat down with God about my diagnosis and medication. The doctor told me that, because of my young age, I needed to change my lifestyle and diet, and then I embarked on this journey of healthy living and eating. I was very lucky because that year I started working in Greenwich and I met my lovely friend Sharon Frieslaar. She was very healthy, practised healthy living and eating and did lots of walking, and that really encouraged me, so I started to change my diet and joined a gym. Lo and behold, I lost a lot of weight; I walked long distances, sometimes from Woolwich centre to Blackheath and sometimes from Woolwich centre to Lee High Road. I varied my journey, so I didn't get bored with my route. It worked, as I lost weight. However, towards the end of my contract with Greenwich, I experienced a lot of losses and deaths in my family, which affected my health routine, and the weight started piling up again.

Interestingly, on Friday, 17 January 2020, Mama Reverend Betty King was praying. She then asked if we could come to the altar around midnight and was praying about blood pressure – I didn't fully engage with the prayer as I had lived with high blood pressure for some time. I was taking medication on and off.

There was a part of me that believed God was going to heal me of high blood pressure because, at some point, my medication had been reduced, so, at the back of my mind, I believed that I would stop taking medication. Something I have lived to regret. Similarly, I was trying to manage it by changing my lifestyle. So collectively, I didn't pray fervently or with vigour when Mama Reverend Betty raised that prayer on the altar. I was reminded of what happened on Friday evening during our Prayer Meeting, where I felt that the prophetess had spiritually discerned that someone was struggling with high blood pressure.

Still, I didn't fully engage in the prayer session.

In the next chapter, I will share what happened.

Where It All Started

> **I shall not die but live, And declare the works of the Lord.
> Psalm 118:17 (NKJV)**

It was one of my normal working-from-home days, and I had my favourite song of the season by Phil Thompson, entitled "My Worship", playing in my head as I was working.

And I will not be silent
I will always worship You
As long as I am breathing
I will always worship You
And I will not be silent
I will always worship You
As long as I am breathing

I will always worship You
And I will not be silent
I will always worship You
As long as I am breathing
I will always worship You

I remember being a bit agitated and upset with an incident in my family that I felt was a demonic attack because somebody had suicidal ideation.

I was preoccupied in my head, stressed about work and timelines, but I was just leaning on God and getting strength from that song on that day. In the midst of working and typing, there was a strange feeling of something strange snapping inside of me, and it felt like there was water dripping on the inside of me – from the middle of my head to the temples. At that point, I realised that something was strange and something had happened. So, I stopped typing. As soon as I stopped, I noticed that my hand was withering, and I said in a loud voice, "No, I cannot be having a stroke!" My hand was getting worse. While observing the hand, I had gotten my legs off the sofa and onto the floor. I just felt my left leg sliding, and the enemy reminded me of that Monster Attack that took my mother out at age 59 (I have chosen to call a stroke a "Monster Attack" because I don't even want to embrace it), and it felt like it wanted to do that for me six years earlier.

At this point, all I could remember was that I would speak to the enemy directly. All that could come to my head was the scripture – *"I shall not die but live and declare the works of the Lord"* (Psalm 118:17). I said it loud, as an outburst. It felt like something was pushing it from the inside of me out to speak it into the atmosphere.

All of this happened so fast. Immediately after the outburst, I felt the song rise in my spirit and started to sing loudly, "I will not be silent. I will always worship you; as long as I am living, I will always worship you." It was my way of talking to God at the time. Tears ran down my cheeks as I continued to sing.

By the time I realised what was happening, I could feel weakness on my whole left side. I could not balance myself or hold my left side up. At this juncture, I felt that I needed to call an ambulance.

While talking to the ambulance crew, I was losing my speech. I explained that I was on my own, and the ambulance crew asked – how would I open the door? At that point, the determination and fearlessness told me that I was going to walk to the door. It hadn't registered with me that I couldn't walk. But I was so determined that I was going to open the door that I started crawling.

I felt defeated when I reached the door because I couldn't stand up. All of this was happening so fast, and I guess I couldn't process what was happening because I wasn't even aware of the enormity of the trauma I had just experienced.

The ambulance crew could sense that and said that I must not worry about the door and that they would kick the door open. My fearless nature returned, and I decided to crawl back to the living room, take the key out of my handbag and throw it onto the balcony. I wasn't going to stop, and that is exactly what I did. The crawling took me back to what had happened in November 2019 when I went on a pilgrimage with the church to Israel, Egypt and Jordan.

My beloved spiritual mother at that time, Mama Reverend Betty King, had walked me to the River Jordan to be baptised by the pastors from the church. I vividly remembered her singing, "I am no longer a slave to fear, I am a child of God", before I was immersed, and her powerful voice reverberated over the atmosphere and into my spirit. It felt like I was living under that prophetic song on the day of the Monster Attack. I was fearless. I was so fearless there was never a single moment or second where I thought I might stop breathing or collapse – God didn't even allow me to think about the extent of the trauma to my brain at the time. I am so grateful that God made my brain function like a child because my brain is normally racing and overthinking, but that day God silenced my racing brain. All I was focusing on was what I had to do next. There was no fear. The whole time from when it first happened to the ambulance was 15 minutes, but it felt like it was in slow motion – like a movie happening in front of me – like I was not part of the experience. The fact that I was so cognisant – to plan, sequence and act on things – even though I had paralysis on my left side – I was able to process things still, and still be on the go.

I know, and I have no doubt in my mind, that God was with me. For me to be on the verge of losing my speech, and that I was able to communicate so well with the ambulance crew until they got me, it could only be God. I can testify the following scripture became so real.

> The pangs of death surrounded me … the snares of death confronted me, in my distress I called upon the Lord and I cried out to my God. He heard

> my voice from his temple and my cry came before him, even to his ears. *(Psalm 18:4-6)*

Another life-threatening incident occurred two months after my discharge.

Excruciating pain in my left leg woke me up, which was the leg affected by the Monster Attack. I took painkillers and struggled to go back to sleep. I managed to sleep. When I woke up, my leg was so swollen, and the pain had now moved to my knee. I had called the ambulance – the first question they asked was: "Was the call related to Covid-19?" When I said no, they said they weren't going to come.

I took painkillers again and managed to doze off to sleep again. When I woke up, the pain was worse. It was in my thigh, and at this point, I struggled to get out of bed. The enemy started to discourage me. "Look at you. You are on your own. You can't even get out of bed to relieve yourself. There is not even someone to get you some water from the kitchen." I think I was broken – I lost a bit of hope, and then I remembered the verse in Psalm 42:9 – where it says, *"I will say to God my Rock, why have you forgotten me?"* I then phoned the ambulance a second time – when the pain was in my hip. I explained to them that the pain was moving and the swelling was getting worse. At that point, I couldn't even get out of bed. I thought if I needed to relieve myself and had to do so on my bed, how my quality of life had depreciated, and I asked myself – "Is this how my life is going to be?" When I spoke to the ambulance a second time, they said they were not coming – the same as before – unless it was Covid, it was a no.

At this time, the church service was starting online for the first time, and I just appreciated that I could be with my church family. God just made the pain subside for me to forget it. As I got involved in worship and the service, Reverend Betty King said the most endearing thing: "Zola, we miss you."

It was a God moment. Immediately when the service ended, my brain switched back to the pain. At this time, my bladder was bursting, and I was hungry and desperate just for someone to help me. At this point, I was moving with a frame and couldn't even reach the Zimmer frame. Then the phone rang. It was like an angel, a lovely, very kind lady from NHS 111. She was reading through my notes – how? I do not know! She said what she had read in my medical notes caused her to worry about me, and she instructed London Ambulance Services to come and assess me. She felt I was high risk as I had just been discharged and was showing worrying symptoms. She said if the ambulance did not turn up in half an hour, I should call her directly. Shortly after we finished talking, the ambulance turned up. Only God!

They took me to the hospital, where I had a scan showing a massive blood clot in my groin. The doctor was very clear that the clot could have been fatal.

How God Revealed Himself

> **Peace I leave with you, My peace I give to you; not as the world gives do I give to you. Let not your heart be troubled, neither let it be afraid.**
> **John 14:27 (NKJV)**

When I got to Princess Royal Hospital, the doctors who carried out my MRI scan explained the process to me. If there was a blockage in my brain, they could unblock that. However, if there had been a haemorrhage, that would be a serious bleed on the brain, and they confirmed after the MRI that it was a haemorrhage. Again, I wasn't scared. The Lord just gave me this sense of peace, and when I recall this, I know that when the Bible says, *"though I walk through the valley of the shadow of death, I will fear no evil. For you are with me. Your rod and your staff, they comfort me"* (Psalm 23:4) – that scripture was so real to me. It just described what had happened. One of the doctors asked me if I was on my own, and I said yes. I knew that at that point, there was an Angelic host with me when the incident happened as I lived on my own.

The weight of God's presence during this traumatic ordeal was palpable, especially when I got to the ward because I observed everybody around me was "nil by mouth". It still hadn't registered with me that the Monster Attack should have affected the muscles in my neck. Supernaturally it didn't. I was able to eat. A young man was admitted a few hours after me. Very healthy-looking, we had a bit of a chat. And that was the time that I decided it was a Monster Attack. He was just like me – going about his business, then he had an attack. And sadly, he passed away in the early hours of that morning.

The nurses were trying to protect me, and then I guess I was affected by what happened. I guess God has a sense of humour – it felt like half of my body was lifeless – and I was carrying death, and there was a death in the ward. However, through God's sense of humour, people on the ward snored, and I thought, "I am still in the land of the living."

I might have been carrying a lifeless side of my body, but I was still in the land of the living. The different sounds from the snoring ministered to me to tell me that there were living souls. It took me away from the place of darkness and sadness to hope – I was alive and breathing, and that resonated again with my song:

I will not be silent,
I will always worship you,
as long as I am breathing,
I will always worship you.

When I was transferred from Princess Royal Hospital to Lewisham Hospital, the Lord supernaturally provided me with a private room.

Interestingly, on admission to the hospital, the nurse who admitted me sternly remarked that I did not qualify for a private room and that, once there was a space in the ward the next day, I would be transferred to the open ward.

As soon as she closed the door, I said that scripture: "God, when you open a door no man can close it, and when you close a door no man can open it" (Revelation 3:8). Then I claimed that room.

What is to follow is just the goodness of God through His providence, for He gave me that room for the reasons I will explain below.

By the end of that week, I knew there was a purpose – God's purpose in me having that room and not being in an open ward. For it just became a prayer centre. The first shocked response to the miracle happened when a male nurse from Uganda came for routine duty. He was shocked when he saw my beautiful smiling face. His paperwork had prepared him to encounter a more damaged, deformed face, judging from the severity of the stroke. According to him, I should have had a sloping face, my speech should have been badly affected, and he was shocked that it wasn't so. He was a Christian. He started to talk to me about his daughter, who had been so ill that she died, and God miraculously resurrected her.

When he used to talk to God, he used to call Him the God of Miriam – his daughter's name. And when he saw what God had done through me, he said, "Miriam's God is going to be Zola's God."

The next day, Annette from the stroke support unit came to see me, and she had all the notes regarding what had happened. With a quizzical stare, she asked if I was Zola. I responded that I was. Annette did a double take and exclaimed, "I have worked for the stroke support unit for many years, and I have never seen somebody with this stroke level coming out like you." Then she said, "I am not a Christian, the whole thing is confusing and complicated for me, but something has happened to you."

I replied, "I am a Christian, and I am so loved by Jesus, and it is Jesus who has done this for me. If you don't know Jesus and find this confusing for you, look at me and know He is real."

On the same day, the first day, when the physiotherapist and occupational therapist came to assess me, they were baffled because my core was so strong that I could sit up. They just remarked that this was a strange stroke that leaves the face and the neck, affects the arm, leaves the core and the body and then affects the leg. And when they said that, I was reminded of the first night when I was admitted. I observed that everybody in the ward was "nil by mouth", and when the nurse came to speak to me and assess me, I didn't even know that my throat could have been affected. I just knew that I was able to eat. When he said he needed to give me yoghurt as part of the assessment, he explained that the muscles in the neck get affected when you have had a stroke. As a result, you choke – my muscles were not affected. I was the only patient who was able to eat in the ward.

After the first day, God just kept showing up.

I remember, that first evening, I was feeling low, angry, and questioning God, asking him why He had allowed this to happen. The enemy was feeding me with lies. I was thinking about my vulnerability, that I was on my own, and how I would not be able to return to work and make a living as a locum. I remember God saying to me, "I have left you with your voice so that you can engage in warfare. I have preserved your voice as a weapon of warfare, and I want you to use your mouth to decree and declare." At that point, I started talking to my hand. I said to my hand, "the brain cannot tell you what to do because there is a breakdown in my brain. There is no signal for instructions, but you are going to listen to my voice."

I looked at my lifeless, motionless, coal-black hand and said, "Move." The middle fingers began to move. I screamed because I was so shocked and cried, "Lord, I believe, help my unbelief"(Mark 9:24). Interestingly, when the physiotherapist came in the morning, she told me that I needed to speak nicely to my hand and my leg and told me exactly what God had told me before. The brain and hand are not talking to each other. I needed to speak kindly to my hand and leg so that the nerves around the hand could compensate for what the brain would have done.

One morning I was sitting on my bed waiting for breakfast. This beautiful woman came through the door singing, "Your Grace and Mercy brought me through, I am living this moment because of You" – she sang in such a joyful way. It was an old song that I loved, and it ministered to me at that moment. It was like there was an impartation of joy. I sat up, trying to shuffle on my bed, and said, "Who are you?"

Then the room was filled with the presence of God. She said, "There is a watchman here."

We started worshipping with this song and praying until I returned to my senses. I told her to go back and serve others. We had a few of those amazing moments during my stay. She would come back during her lunch breaks, and we would share the Word, pray and worship. She was an amazing worshipper. Then one morning, another beautiful lady came into the room to clean, and I was just led to minister to her, telling her how much God loves her. She became emotional and said she had been involved in a domestic abuse incident that morning. We started talking, and I gave her some advice and counsel. We prayed. She left and came back the next day with the most amazing smile I have ever seen and said that, afterwards, she felt the prayer had shifted things because, when she got home, her husband apologised. She came quite frequently to the room to pray. She was a prayer warrior.

Pastors that came to visit me opened the door for many healthcare assistants who came seeking prayer.

The Hand of God

There was one Sunday when I had four men of God: Pastor Lunga Sazinge, Pastor Mike Sirewu, Pastor Raymond Thorne, and Prophet Roland Harding. We just had a beautiful time of fellowship.

And in that very first week, I cannot forget this experience; I am still amazed and in awe of God. I am still desperate for this to happen again because it was the first time I had a vision. It had to take me having a Monster Attack to have a vision, I guess, because, at that time, God was my all. There was nothing in me except for God. That particular morning, in the early hours of the morning, I had a vision of a pure white lamb with very clear eyes, whose ears were lying very flat but very attentive. It was lying on the bed rail. And it was just so peaceful. I did not want to move my fingers or breathe because, if I made any movement, I felt the lamb was going to leave. I was so desperate for the lamb to stay forever; I did not want it to move. It was the most beautiful, divine encounter.

I was part of the ensemble Gospel choir at Emmanuel Church in Lee. The love that I experienced from the choir members was unbelievable – but even from people who were not part of the choir, for example, Dr Agyekum (we had ministered in music for his 70th birthday a month before). When he heard that I was in Lewisham Hospital, he turned up ten minutes before the end of the visiting time, and the nurses allowed him to stay a little bit longer, and he just brought in the presence of God. We had a fantastic time of fellowship, and he strengthened me. Uncle Paul Lunga and Aunty Stella, his wife, (leaders of the Ensemble choir) went out of their way for me. Aunty Stella would squeeze time in between work commitments to come and see me.

Sister Vera brought in so much love and strengthened me. Then Brother Salleh, who was not even an ensemble member, came to see me with some people. And he said, "We thought we had come to encourage you, but we left encouraged."

I was upbeat and in high spirits, and I knew when he said that it was because God had given me peace.

Buyiswa (my big sissy) sent me a voice note that touched me when she was in South Africa. She said she was woken up by God at 3.00 a.m. to pray for me. The thought that occurred in her mind was that maybe God had boasted to the enemy about me, as he did with Job. She said she wanted me to cling to God. It felt like she was in the UK because we spoke more than when she was in the country. It was really about believing and trusting in God and believing that this, too, shall come to pass.

Divine Support / Truthvine Family Church Support

> **Therefore I say to you, do not worry about your life, what you will eat or what you will drink; nor about your body, what you will put on. Is not life more than food and the body more than clothing? Look at the birds of the air, for they neither sow nor reap nor gather into barns; yet your heavenly Father feeds them. Are you not of more value than they?**
> **Matthew 6:25-26 (NKJV)**

I know that my steps were ordered by the Lord to Truthvine Church. Let me emphasise that this is a family church which became a family in every sense of the word. I don't have family in the UK, but I felt loved, nurtured, supported and valued. I can confidently say that, without the amount of love, care and support I experienced from the church, I would not have come this far in my recovery.

Reverend Betty, who I affectionately called Mama, has been more than a spiritual covering for me. From day one, she asked one of the pastors to anoint me with oil shortly after the Monster Attack. *"Is anyone among you sick? Let him call for the elders of the church, let them pray over him, anointing him with oil in the name of the Lord"* (James 5:14). It was only when I returned to the church, I realised that Reverend Betty had been discreet about the illness. She believed that I needed to be protected and for the leadership to pray for me.

Mama, Reverend Betty, the mighty woman of God, would be on the phone whenever I was admitted to the hospital. She continuously reassured me, saying, "This too shall come to pass."

I was so touched by her mother's heart and kindness. I remember receiving a text message from her, asking me whether the financial gift she wanted to sow into my life was sufficient. I thought the last zero was a typing error, and I was lost for words when I received the amount. I have experienced nothing but love and kindness from Mama Reverend Betty; what a caring and generous soul!

One time, I reacted to the blood-thinning medication and was admitted to the hospital. Reverend Betty was quicker than Usain Bolt in calling the doctors to get information and understand my treatment. I was unaware of how far Mama Betty had gone in her motherly role; it was only after I returned to church that she shared what had happened. I welled up with tears thinking – what manner of love is this?

She ensured that I received all the support I needed by asking one of the sisters in the church to assist with cleaning, cooking and driving me to church when my health improved. She asked hospitality team members to ensure that I was provided with food.

The people the church appointed to support me have done so with excellence, consistency and intentionality. Sister Angela would come – not only to do the shopping for me – but also to do personal beautification treatments like pedicures and manicures. She would also do my hair and cook for me and

– without fail – picked me up for prayers and to attend church, and this was done with so much love and with a servant's heart.

Olukemi was just touched by God to offer help to me. She was not asked by the church but helped out of the kindness of her heart. Her level of commitment and consistency touched me so deeply. I experienced so much love and care; she felt like a daughter I never had. I will talk more about this when I am talking about the level of support I received from the children that have become closer to me over the years – including my friend's children.

TRUTHVINE CHURCH – Returning to Church:

I decided to start going to church as soon as a bit of my mobility was restored. And I was very mindful that there is no lift in church. However, I was just so determined to go as the longer I stayed at home, the more the enemy would feed me with lies. I trusted God that I would be able to do the stairs. Going up the stairs was a bit of a struggle, and coming down was just not doable. I was reminded that, shortly before the start of the lockdown, the physiotherapy assistant was trying to help me learn to walk down the stairs outside the block. There was a mishap where she was not confident in the strategy, and I landed on the stairs on my bottom. I was so frightened, and it replayed in my mind when I tried to do that in church. In her mothering way, Mama Reverend Betty was not having any of it. She had already lined up men from the church to carry me down the stairs (they put me on a chair and carried me down the flight of stairs). The pride in me was like – I don't want to see that happening, but because she is such an authoritarian figure – she was very clear that this was her instruction and is what needs to happen.

Reflecting on that, it was such a humbling experience of brotherly love – when the Bible talks about being each other's keepers, everyone was keen to help. They were not even bothered that I am not a small person – so carrying me down the stairs was not for the fainthearted, but they did it so well. At some point, my flesh panicked, thinking, what if they dropped me? The level of love I have personally experienced from the church is indescribable.

During my recovery period, I attended the "When Strong Women Unite" (Women's ministry) meeting and the day's topic was "breaking strongholds of the mind". It felt as if the sickness was intended to transport me back to my childhood and for the Spirit of the Lord to help me deal with unresolved emotional traumas which have been a hindrance over the years and kept me bound.

Additionally, the session mentioned above led to me asking forgiveness from people I had hurt in the past (my ex-husband and his partner, my best friend's sister – I had been dishonest with money and paid it back; my Aunty – I confronted her for lack of integrity as the family had appointed her to be an executor for my cousin's estate, and she embezzled the funds and I accused her of witchcraft due to her heartless actions; I had to ask for forgiveness because it was not my place to judge her).

The other significant session from the Women's ministry was dealing with "unblocking plumb lines". Being out of work allowed me to spend time with God and ponder on some of the issues triggered by this session. The raw and painful emotions manifesting through anger regarding my absent father resurfaced. I can only testify that what the enemy intended for evil, God turned out for good. I made contact with my paternal family, met my aunt for the first time when I travelled abroad and visited my late father's grave for closure.

The church became the hands, feet and arms of Jesus in my life. I have not only received physical healing through nurturing and love, but I have also been healed emotionally.

The Children

> " ... more are the children of the desolate Than the children of the married woman," says the Lord.
> Isaiah 54:1, last part (NKJV)

Over the years, the Lord added children into my life. I don't have children of my own. They have all played such an amazing role from the outset until now. I then realised through my healing process that their names are very prophetic.

Out of their love, kindness, and impact on my healing journey, I sense that another book was birthed regarding childlessness. I will cover the impact of childless-ness extensively in a separate book.

Ada – (her name means the first daughter) went the extra mile. She left everything and focused on supporting me. On day one, she picked up my Bible and Holy Communion emblems from home. Ada and her mother cooked for me. She did my laundry with her parents' support, ensuring I had clean clothes all the time. Ada wasted no time in challenging Lewisham Hospital staff if she perceived any neglect in their care of me. The senior staff knew who she was. I affectionately call her brown sugar. She explained to the staff that I was her second mother. Ada is a warrior like me.

Interestingly, when one of the pastors first saw her, they walked behind her and described her as speedy Gonzalez. She was actively involved in the whole process – preparation for my discharge, the delivery of special equipment, and all the arrangements involved. She arranged for a cleaner to clean my home to make it comfortable before my discharge.

I remember her saying I was her Valentine's date as I was discharged on Valentine's Day. The amount of love and dedication that I experienced touched my heart. She continuously said I had always been there for her family when I tried to thank her. "*He who waters others will himself be watered*" (Proverbs 13:25).

She was even helping me with really looking at how I was going to manage my finances. We looked at how we could cancel things that were not necessary. The level of encouragement I received from her kept me going. What was interesting was when she saw my women's study Bible – unbeknown to me, she bought herself the same study Bible. We had a deeper spiritual journey together – discussing specific spiritual subjects mentioned in that Bible – such as purity, young women and marriage – all the issues affecting young women. I have seen a lot of growth in her spiritual walk and how this study Bible has triggered an interest within her to read the Word and get more understanding.

Art Michael Junior – Ada's brother, who I affectionately call "Mkhulu" – means grandfather (he is a deep thinker and has a caring nature). When he became aware of what had happened, he decided, without telling anybody, that he was going to do the shopping for me. At this point, I didn't know how much my illness had affected him. Apparently, he was so sad, and I think it was because he knew I am on my own. I remember when I was readmitted to the hospital around Easter, he would call to check how I was doing. He is not a person who always phoned family and significant others, but I witnessed an endearing level of love and kindness. He would check to get an update on me, constantly asking if they were looking after me well. During the lockdown, Ada visited me, and she called him on a video call. It was so sweet as I was standing on the balcony with him having a video call because he insisted that he wanted to see me.

Going back to the shopping, when Ada brought the shopping, Mkhulu drove from Southampton, bringing the shopping. His mother informed me that when he bought the shopping, she wanted to keep some of the stuff, but Art Michael was clear that I could not go out and do the shopping and I should be the priority to get more. I have never seen so much food shopping. It was like he was shopping for a small army, not for only one person! The level of generosity made Philippians 4:19, "But my God shall supply all your needs according to His riches in glory by Christ Jesus", so alive and so real. There was so much overflow; it was not only food – there were sanitisers, wipes, a range of supplements – not just small size, everything was in abundance. Again when I expressed my gratitude to him, his response was the same as Ada's.

Bongo, my friend's son, means "pride"; he is our pride. When he visited me at the hospital, he looked so sad and referred to the time when he had his coming-of-age ceremony in South Africa. He didn't know I was in the country. He was covered in a blanket when I walked into the room. I began praying, and he recognised my voice. So, when he came to visit me at the hospital, he was so sad and said, "how could this happen to my Aunty?" I just reminded him that his Aunty is a praying warrior.

"I know, Aunty, you are my second mother," he replied. In time both he and Ada said the same thing. It was like God was reminding me that I was not childless. Through the Monster Attack, God reminded me I was not childless; I was a mother of many.

Mihlali – "Excitement" – I affectionately call her Tutu; she brought in so much joy and happiness when she came to see me at the hospital. She reminded me of when I just turned up at her house at 6:00 a.m. to pray with her when she turned 18. I did not have any gift for her – *"silver and gold I do not have but what I do have I give you ...*" (Acts 3:6) – I just brought her the Word and blessings of the Lord that were in my heart because I just needed to do that. She remembered that.

Olukemi – "God cares for me" – Olukemi has lived out her prophetic name in my life. She allowed herself to be used by God to care for me. I did not anticipate our relationship would develop the way it has, at the beginning of my healing journey. Interestingly from the beginning, I became aware that I was three years younger than her mother, so this developed into a mother-daughter relationship. She allowed herself to be used by God to birth this testimony. She just put the book into a structure – brought it to life – as a result, when we first had the conversation, I could feel something had been triggered inside of me, and I started writing that night. The writing fulfilled the prophetic words I had received regarding books I needed to write. Mama – Reverend Betty King – confirmed that I should write on my return to church. Olukemi – I affectionately call her princess Kemzi. She has brightened dark days during this journey, and her level of generosity and kindness has exceeded my expectations. She became a daughter that I never had. From basic chores to immaculate house cleaning every week, intensive prayers, and her consistency and level of intentionality, I have never experienced such a level of love and commitment. Someone who is not family showing the love of Jesus – pure love, and I just knew that if things needed to be done at short notice, like DWP or GP forms, Kemzi would do that with a smile. This book would not have been completed without Kemzi's help;

she sacrificed her spare time from her hectic schedule to be my scribe because I have weakness in my left arm.

Hergy – we just connected at a deep level when I returned to the church. I had known him before, and we had a special connection on the first day he came to church. Our closeness got stronger when I returned to the church; he had changed so much, seasoned, confident, and just overall beautiful and gorgeous. We became very close, and during one of his prophetic insight moments, he talked about the scripture in the book of Genesis when Jacob wrestled with the Angel of the Lord, and he felt that is what I could be going through. As I continued attending church, he talked about how my fighting attitude and spirit had encouraged him and gave me that sense of just fighting and continuing to fight.

Little ones from church are generally very sweet and adorable; however, when I went back to church, some of them were prophetic. This particular incident stands out. The little person took my walking stick and waited for me at the top of the stairs. She moved towards the door as soon as I got to the top of the stairs. She looked me in the eye with the most delightful smile, beckoning me to follow her. I had no option but to comply; she would take a few steps as I got closer to her. We reached my special chair, and my footstool was folded next to the chair; she unfolded it and what amazed me was she took off my shoes (she had seen adults doing that). She then placed her hand on her hip, beaming with delight as if to say, "Look, we have done it!"

On another occasion, one child rushed to open a door for me; she hugged me, saying, "Aunty, you will run and dance again; don't worry."

I had another one telling me that she had picked a flower for me and had forgotten it in her parents' car. I was so touched by the little people's kind gestures.

Sisterhood and Family

> Be hospitable to one another without grumbling. As each one has received a gift, minister it to one another, as good stewards of the manifold grace of God.
> 1 Peter 4:9-10 (NJKV)

Ntombehlubi – "Ntomby". I have known her through a friend; we were not close before I became unwell. I was amazed by how God used her to support me. She became a close big sister. Ntomby stayed with me from the time I was discharged – the first night I was discharged, Ntomby was here. She carries the fruits of the spirit – joy, kindness, happiness, and so much joy and laughter around her. Serious things were just dealt with in a joyful way that you don't even feel the pain or depth of what you are going through because of her sense of humour.

In the beginning, I didn't understand the extent of my illness and how it would impact my day-to-day functioning. Without Ntomby's support – I don't think I would have survived the first few days; it was hard (following the discharge.) For example, I was provided with a hospital bed. I didn't conceptualise the fact that my urinary system was weak and was affected by the Monster Attack. I had quite a few accidents that used to upset me as it made me realise the quality of my life had changed. I got overwhelmed, thinking that this was going to be my life. Ntomby would make it sound so light and easy – she dealt with the situation so well. If I wet myself and she had to change my underwear, she would do it so jokingly, that I would laugh myself, between the tears. She would make me feel like it is a passing phase and part of the after-effects of the Monster Attack. Her nursing background helped a lot. One day, she had to go to work at night, early evening – 6.00 p.m. to 11.00 p.m. I was in a state of despair and fear because I couldn't even transfer from bed to the commode at that time. I couldn't sleep, and I felt as if I was under oppression. At some point that evening, it felt like a shadow was standing in the hallway. I couldn't even get out of bed to turn the lights on – I felt so much alone. However, I determined that, if she didn't turn up that night, I would stay awake and pray. In the midst of that, 2.00 a.m. – I heard someone punching the codes on the key safe, and it was her. She had travelled all the way to look after me as she was worried. She has been such a gift!

Doreen, I have known her for almost 30 years. We worked together in social care abroad before we relocated to the UK. She has always been like an anchor in my life and kind of my "go-to" person. When I met her, I was newly qualified. Everybody I knew within our professional fraternity would speak of her as a prayer warrior. I have experienced that throughout different journeys in my life.

She left her family and stayed with me for two days, shortly after I was discharged from the hospital. She cleaned my house and changed my bedding. I had been struggling with filling in the form for the DWP – it is quite a lengthy, detailed document; she was not fazed. And interestingly, despite what she does with her work, she works with adults; she was so concerned about the fact that I live on my own and asked if I would consider moving to Surrey with her family for a while.

She encouraged me in the Lord, sharing the Word and strengthening me. She is just a very energetic and positive person. Even after she left, she sent me scriptures and anything to make me optimistic. She sowed into my life financially.

Zuki – I have known her for about 20 years. She lives and works in Wales. She visited whilst I was in the hospital. She drove a round trip of 12 hours the same day just to see how I was. What level of sacrifice? She brought me South African goodies and made me feel like I was back home. When I got discharged, she came and stayed with me for about four days. I didn't even know that she was a stroke nurse. And unlike my friend Ntomby, she was pushing me to be independent and came with a completely different approach. For example, one day, she returned and brought me some T-shirts and explained that I needed to change into proper clothing after bathing, because if I continued to wear my pyjamas during the day, I would feel more poorly. She explained that I would feel much better if I wore regular clothes. I noticed the difference. She stayed in the same room with me, slept on the sofa and kept an eye on me. However, she was very strategic and would pretend to be asleep when I was struggling to go on the commode to make sure I was getting more independent. She changed the rules when she came. She was very authoritarian. Both nurses – Ntomby and Zuki – are very different characters and had different approaches to my care.

Michelle – I call her my sister from another mother. She is an amazing person and woman of God from the

Gambia. She is very kind, upfront and generous. She always told me that I needed to leave work and go and work in the vineyard and the Lord will provide for me. When she visits, she brings the whole market. She brought the things I needed. She knew which ones to get for me – it was like it was in her head. Everything was done in large quantities. Sometimes I had to remind her that I was on my own. She was very encouraging and always reminded me how much God loves me. Even when she travelled to the Gambia for Christmas, she called me to check how I was doing and reminded me that this shall come to pass.

Patricia – I call her "Vuyo" – the one who brings joy. She is always wearing a smile, full of joy and very kind. When I was in the hospital, she brought in all the toiletries, the yellow scrubbing things, the wet wipes, things you often forget. Even when she did that, it was in abundance. When I was discharged, my freezer was just full of cooked healthy food. Some were Nigerian, and some were from her nutritionist. She made fresh smoothies with ginger, turmeric and healthy stuff, less sugar but delicious.

Sandra – my prayer warrior, she does not finish a sentence without mentioning the Lord and His goodness. She carries the presence of God. I remember her first hospital visit, she changed the atmosphere as soon as she walked through the door, and we had mighty visitation. Sandra has a very calm demeanour, strong faith, nurturing and generosity. She used my healing testimony to strengthen and give hope to others before this book was finalised.

Mpumi – she is more than a friend. She was in anguish when she became aware of what had happened. We have supported each other practically, financially and spiritually over the years. She touched me so deeply when she said our circle of friends should be making plans to come to England from South Africa to support me. Mpumi gives selflessly, and she made time to call me frequently despite her losses and personal tragedies.

Family – my family did not fully comprehend the seriousness of the Monster Attack because my speech had not been affected. Only my younger sister understood the seriousness of my illness because she is a nurse. We explored whether an extended family member could travel to the UK to care for me. However, Covid happened, and we had to abandon the plans. My cousins, Lulu, Thami, and Tantaswa, were on the phone frequently checking on me. They were all finding it difficult because they couldn't offer practical support as they all live abroad.

Being Used Amidst Adversity

> **And everyone who was in distress, everyone who was in debt, and everyone who was discontented gathered to him.**
> **1 Samuel 22:2 (NKJV)**

I had two healthcare assistants who stayed with me for two weeks when Ntomby returned to work. They were live-in carers – generously provided by Norma, one of my sisters from church. I must admit that I received the best Healthcare Assistants (their names shall remain anonymous). The second one carried the presence of God. The joy of the Lord radiated from her. At her request, we did Bible studies in the evenings. Then one day, she started telling me about her life's journey.

She would travel between islands in the Caribbean and trade. When she settled in the UK, she would leave her home every morning to travel to central London to run a sewing business. As she spoke, I could see the character of the virtuous woman in Proverbs 31. I started to share that scripture with her verse by verse and how it related to her practice. She became so emotional, remarking that she had heard that scripture before; however, when I shared it with her, it became so alive, and she could relate. Often, during our times together, her daughter and husband would call and tell her how much they missed her hospitality. The following verse describes her relationship with her family: *"Her children rise up and call her blessed, her husband also, and he praises her"* (Proverbs 31:28). She was sent as a blessing and found me to be a blessing to her. That is just like our loving Father.

Ntomby's testimony: One evening, when Ntomby was with me, she began to ask questions about Jesus and the Bible. She wanted to know how I learned to pray, using the words of the Bible. Judging by her questions, I sensed the Holy Spirit hovering and nourishing her heart for more of God. Immediately, Galatians 5:22 came to mind about the fruits of the Spirit. I felt this was speaking about her character. She remarked that caring for me had opened her eyes to see the goodness of God and how He provided for people who knew Him personally. She had seen the kind of people who came to visit me and the abundant provision of God in my life. There was the miracle of my speedy recovery and the strength I showed in trusting God amid this adversity – just trusting God. She made this profound statement: "I feel that God has sent me to you to witness the word of God becoming alive."

Interestingly, months later, she came to share the Word with me!

A few days later, a lovely healthcare assistant came to my home. We were getting ready for my shower, and I complimented her on her looks. She dressed well, and her clothes were always very well coordinated. As soon as I gave her this compliment, what she did next shocked me. She started to get very emotional and pulled up her blouse. She was covered in bruises. She talked about experiencing very worrying levels of domestic violence and sadistic behaviour from the perpetrator. She was scared and didn't want the police or social services to become involved. It was clear to me that there would not be any support for me and that this was her moment to receive much-needed guidance. She was my assignment for that day. I stepped out of the role of a patient and into that of a social worker, explaining the importance of having both the police and social services on board and the huge ramifications not doing so would have on her child's future. I was relieved when she consented to inform the police and social services. I called them as soon as I could. I don't know what happened to her, since I never saw her again. I hoped and prayed that she was placed in a refuge.

Whilst I was still in hospital, in the early days of my admission, I was still very poorly. Another acquaintance visited me, which is something that I expected as she is a very kind person. She started talking about quite intense personal issues that she was struggling with then and was very animated and upset. I could feel what she was saying affecting me as I was very poorly at that point, so I gently asked her to leave because she was making me worse. I asked her, "Why would you leave your home, come to the hospital and share such disturbing family issues?"

She said I was the only person whom she could trust. I kindly asked her to leave. When I returned home, she came again. On the day she returned, the Lord reminded me of 1 Kings 22:2. King David was running away from Saul and hiding in the cave of Adullam. The scripture captured my attention because it talks about the issues David experienced. Interestingly, the same day someone else came to visit and shared the same scripture with me. It felt to me that I was in my little cave with my illness, and it felt like people were coming to seek advice despite my struggles with my health.

The Lord continued to use me when I was admitted the second time (around Easter time with a clot). I was placed in a small ward with three elderly patients; the youngest was in her mid-eighties. I had the courage to minister to them, especially to the oldest in her nineties, and she did not take kindly to the fact that I introduced Christ into our conversation. The lady in her mid-eighties was receptive, and I led her to Christ, to God be the glory! Interestingly, they were all transferred to another hospital literally after we finished. It felt like I was admitted into that ward for that one soul.

Divine Helpers

> **And my God shall supply all your need according to his riches in glory by Christ Jesus.**
> **Philippians 4:19 (NKJV)**

Pastor Raymond – oh my goodness – this is my brother in the Lord. He carries the love of Jesus. He was consistent. He would visit me in the hospital, pray with me, and remind me of how much God loves me and how the enemy would make me focus on the affliction. He has been used so immensely by God during this season. I remember one day when it was still tough for me; my mobility was very limited – maybe 10–15 per cent. That day I was under depression and oppression; I felt so discouraged and alone because I had an accident in the kitchen with food spilt on the floor. The weak left arm was wobbly – it hit something, and the food fell on the floor. It took me to a place of despair, discouragement and hopelessness. The enemy was really on my mind that day with all the lies. Lies of being on my own, nobody to rescue me – it was one of those dark moments. I felt so discouraged and unsure how I would go on. Then God sent Pastor Raymond. I went to bed in tears, very broken. I was in a state of despair, lost hope – he called me, and I wallowed in self-pity – I didn't want to be rescued. I just wanted to wallow in my self-pity. He was persistent, and I told him I didn't want to get out of bed, it was a struggle, but he was having none of it. He was so persistent. It was like

God had told him not to let go of me that day. He came, met me at the door and handed me an envelope. Outside the envelope, the message was "my dearest sister Zola, stand on Psalm 91". And he had sown a seed – I broke down when he left because it felt like God was saying, "*What is man that You are mindful of him, and the son of man that You visit him?*" (Psalm 8:4).

Pastor Raymond would call me; even when he visited his ill father in Barbados, he would call me and still sow into my life. What kind of love is that? He would visit with his lovely wife, Sister Alison, and they brought messages of hope and reminded me of my value and assignment within the kingdom of God. They have been such a huge blessing in my life during this season. On my 20th anniversary in the UK, he bought me *The 40 Day Soul Fast* by Dr Cindy Trimm – this book is such a blessing.

It talks not about what you are eating but what is eating you – emotional wellbeing.

On 21 June, he was used immensely. I decided I wanted to recommit myself to attending Tuesday Prayer meetings. I was contemplating how I would afford the trips to church because I needed taxis to take me there, which are expensive. However, I made that commitment to God that I was going to start my routine again.

I got a phone call from Pastor Raymond out of the blue. I didn't even know he was back from Barbados. He came with his usual smiley, joyful, larger-than-life self. We prayed, and shortly before he left, he sowed exactly £50 into my life, the amount of money I needed to go to church! For the first time, I asked him the name of his church. It is called Wells of Life International

Ministry. He and his wife have been a well of life to me.

Pastor Tabisa Xentsa – she is serving at Ruach church. This mighty woman of God was used in a very special way. I received a call from her on the second or third day following the Monster Attack, and I noticed she was calling me on a video call. As soon as I answered, she said, "Is that you, Zola?" I was shocked because she called me on a video call. Before she asked me, I heard her praying for healing, and I had said "Amen." She asked the second time if it was me. Her question confused me because she had called me. She then said she was going to call me back. When she called back, she explained she was visiting one of the church members with another pastor, who was in hospital, in the Kilburn area. On the way to hospital, she was reading a message I sent her, which she found encouraging, on WhatsApp. Apparently, when she got to the hospital, she put her phone down and started praying for that individual. She believes that while they were holding hands, one of the hands may have accidentally called me on a video call whilst they were praying. And we both felt that God wanted me to be part of that prayer. And by hook or by crook, I needed to be part of that prayer. She didn't even know I was in the hospital and had had a Monster Attack.

Sharon, where do I start with Sharon? She has just been a blessing. I am ever so grateful that she invited me to Truthvine Church, which was like family. I remember when she first visited me the day after I was discharged. She was a good cook and prepared a meal for me, and my friends looked after me. She is such a hospitable person but not a hugging person; unlike me, she never uses affectionate names but has such a deep sense of love in her. So, when she came to cook, she brought me dark chocolate as she is a healthy eater. However, when she left, she asked me if I had eaten my chocolate, which was a bit strange, and I said no. The next day the question came again, and it was the same answer. I think, at this time, she lost the will to live. She said, "You need to open the chocolate", sternly. I was getting irate as I had just been discharged and wondered what was so special about this chocolate. In the end, I obliged and opened the chocolate. In her nicest, sweetest way, she had folded £100 worth of notes inside the chocolate. That was so special! She would come to cook for me after church, finish church late and cook meals that would last for the week. Sometimes she would drive early and drop meals off for me. She sowed love and generosity financially and spiritually in my life and lifted me during weak moments. Very encouraging. She was the person who called my family on the day as she was one of the first people who came to see me in the hospital. She had the daunting task of speaking to my younger sister and telling her what had happened. She is a woman full of the Word of God and encourages you to strengthen yourself in the Lord.

Pastor Fresia – what a gift. A woman of few words. Fountain of Wisdom. Very maternal and nurturing. She was there on day one under the instruction of the senior pastor to go and anoint me. Regular hospital visits, words of wisdom, advising me to be discerning and alert in the Spirit regarding who visits. She sometimes came to bring me food from church, sit with me, and check how I was doing. I was so amazed and touched when she even offered to plait my hair on one occasion. Pastor Fresia is a woman of God I hold in such high esteem, but her level of humility and service just touched me. It just made me feel like I have a family away from family. Very consistent – straight from work to the hospital. There has never been a time when she promised that she was going to visit and didn't turn up, despite the fact she was juggling so many things. She's just one of those people who made me forget that I don't have family in the UK.

Norma – my dearest sister. She has been such a blessing. I didn't know until I had gone back to the church that she had asked somebody that they should intercede for me together. She is like a deadly assassin in prayer. She is very petite but is a powerful warrior when it comes to prayer. I remember a few days after my discharge from the hospital; she was constantly on the phone. One time, it was the early morning hours, and I was half asleep because I was heavily medicated. She called, saying that the Lord had reminded her of something shared by one of her friends who told her that God had spoken to him, saying that we need to remember that it is not prayer alone that people need. This message led her to think about how she could assist me. She generously provided me with a live-in healthcare assistant for two weeks, which I needed. I didn't know at that time how much support I needed because I wasn't aware that I would need this much assistance because of the nature of my paralysis. She sowed into my life: financially, with her time, prayer, and kindness.

Aunty Charity Agyang is a Ghanaian woman of fire. I met this petite dynamo at Ellel Ministries in 2015. She was one of the teachers, and I was part of one of the ministry groups she facilitated. She heard from my precious sister Sandra that I had just come out of the hospital, and interestingly, she had relocated to Ghana. However, she was back in the UK for a medical appointment. She should have left the UK a week before I was discharged, and her appointment was cancelled, so she came to see me. She visited me in February 2020, the same month she had prayed for my emotional healing at Ellel Ministries four years previously. She has an amazing sense of humour, an additional gift for those vessels chosen for healing ministry. When she came to see me, she prayed. We found ourselves laughing because she said, "Satan, you just heard the number five (which is my house number); you didn't even check if it was fifteen or twenty-five – you came to number five, which is the number for Grace, and because there is the number for Grace here, faith has risen!" What was profound, my friend Ntomby who is relatively new in the Christian walk, could feel the presence of God when Sandra and Aunty Charity were praying.

I have observed something from these mighty women of God from Ghana – power and a sense of excellence. I had just come out of the hospital and was fretting about whether I would be able to make it as I depended on people for my care. I was panicking, wondering whether I would be ready for her at 10.00 a.m. as I needed help to get ready. But she was here at 10.00 a.m. There is a spirit of excellence. Even when she left the UK and returned to Ghana, I received a few phone calls that were very calm and reassuring. She would say God has preserved you, and you will pull through.

Pastor Lunga – this young evangelist has just been part of my journey even before I became unwell. He and his wife came with so much joy. His wife is a worshipper. She would always break out in song and worship God in the hospital. Their love kept me standing.

Nolitha is a mighty woman of God. Nothing else comes out of her mouth except for the goodness of God. She has a gift of giving and charity – she gives of her time and her resources, and the number of times she called me in the first stages of my illness touched me. She called daily and assured me of the intercession and that she trusted God for my healing. Interestingly, that level of love and commitment did not waver throughout my healing process.

Even at a time when she was losing friends through Covid, I was also on her mind and in her prayers.

Pastor Mawuli Doe of Kingswood Community Baptist Church has been among other people who were touched to sow into my life. I visited Kingswood Baptist church at the invitation of my beloved sister, Sandra. The church contacted me a few days before Christmas and sowed a significant seed into my life. Their love gift left me speechless.

The South African Fellowship in the UK – I was really touched when the fellowship sent me Christmas shopping on two days before Christmas as I am not a member of the fellowship. I had so much food supply, and my tiny apartment looked like a warehouse. I shared my excess supply with neighbours who had no recourse to public funds.

God Sustained Me Throughout the Journey

> "For I will restore health to you
> And heal you of your wounds,"
> says the Lord.
> Jeremiah 30:17 (NKJV)

Looking at this whole journey, I was just amazed that in the valley of Baca, in the valley of weeping, there were so many fountains sprinkling my soul, spirit, and physical body, because I have received so many compliments talking about how youthful I look. It's like I have been through a process of renewal.

Spiritually, the Word has become real. The provision God has given me through His faithful sons and daughters has been mind-blowing. It makes me feel like Elijah when the ravens fed him by the brook Cherith.

God has just provided me with the best. Things I could not afford when I was working – food from Waitrose and Marks and Spencer's became my staple food. God has been so specific in terms of my needs. For example, I don't drink dairy milk, and just like that, I get cartons of almond and oat milk (from Truthvine Church – hallelujah!) that covered me for a month. The days when I would look at my healthy breakfast, lunch and meals and one day I had tears flowing through my eyes thinking – look at God, look at the provision from God!

Spiritually, because before the Monster Attack, my brain would be clogged by so many things, and my brain would be so distracted. Then I realised that one evening I would read scripture only once, then in the middle of the night, when I woke up to relieve myself, the scripture would come back so vividly without memorising it. It was like my brain was being renewed. Cognitively I am sharper than I was before I became unwell.

Those around me involved in the medical field – Ntomby, for example – have remarked on how quickly I have recovered, given the seriousness of the stroke I experienced.

Looking back, I have come a long way. While in hospital, I insisted that I wanted to be taken to the toilet for my dignity. The nurses felt I should use a bed pan as all the other patients did. However, I was conscious of the fact that I had no privacy in the ward. I begged to be allowed to go to the bathroom.

Eventually, they used a hoist to take me to the bathroom. I felt like a sack of potatoes being dangled over the toilet pan as they tried to position me on the toilet. I broke down in tears as I realised how dependent I was on others for what was previously a simple, uncomplicated, everyday activity.

My determination meant that the medical team had to think again about how I was being looked after. My choices, wishes and desires had to be taken into account. The nurses arranged for the physiotherapist to see me and recommended using a Sara Stedy to aid transportation to the bathroom.

Bed baths were difficult for me. Some nurses were not as thorough with cleansing as they should be. I would be left feeling dirty and smelling. One nurse who came in the evening saw that I had not been cleaned properly and took me to the bathroom to have a shower. It was lovely, even though I had to be supervised during the process. I then asked to be taken to the bathroom so that I could wash myself. One nurse felt it was her duty to let me know that they did not have time to pander to my wishes, but I insisted that I could wash, with help to get to the bathroom. In the end, I was supported towards my independence, and it helped my self-esteem and supported my healing.

It may seem like this was stubbornness on my part, but in my mind, I knew progression would come from practice. Practice would build strength, and I could return to independence in using the bathroom.

I came home in a wheelchair and was provided with a hospital bed which was placed in my living room along with a commode. My living room became my hospital room at home. It was only a short distance from the living room to the bathroom, but I could not walk there. I had to be taken on a Sara Stedy.

When God says in His Word, "Peace I leave with you, not as the world gives do I give to you" (John 14:27), I have experienced his inner peace, even during pain, chaos and confusion.

What the enemy intended for evil, God turned it for good. From this traumatic experience, God made it possible for me to connect with my paternal family in a very God-orchestrated way. I met them in person for the very first time when I travelled abroad. Meeting them has definitely been significant emotional healing for me. I had a deep wound due to rejection by my father. I will discuss this in detail in a separate book.

It was also an opportunity for me to get godly counselling, which I could not do when I was working. Counselling has helped me to put lingering emotional wounds and childhood trauma to rest. Some of the wounds that I had are now being healed. As God is healing me physically, he has also orchestrated emotional healing. In times of adversity, we need to rest in God and believe in His Word that he will never leave us or forsake us (Hebrews 13:5).

I am amazed at what God has done through this healing process. People say that I do not look like I am recovering from a stroke; I look like someone who has had a hip replacement. It is undoubtedly the hand of God. He alone can be praised for what has happened. From the beginning, there were signs that God was helping me, giving me strength when I shouldn't have had the strength and allowing me to be able to eat when others around me could not. He gave me a spirit of independence and determination that helped me to overcome, and pushed staff to do the extra that facilitated my recovery. God does not do half-jobs, so I know He is still working on my case, and in the end, I can lift my voice and raise my hands in total praise to my heavenly Father and friend for the great things He has done!

The Father Heart of God

> **I will be a Father to you, And you shall be My sons and daughters, Says the Lord Almighty.**
> **2 Corinthians 6:18 (NKJV)**

The Monster Attack occurred two months before the first lockdown of the Covid-19 pandemic. By the time the country had come to a standstill, it felt like I was already hidden in Goshen

> *And in that day, I will set apart the land of Goshen, in which my people dwell, that no swarms of flies shall be there in order that you may*

know that I am the Lord.
(Exodus 8:22)

because I was going through my rehabilitation. It was a very challenging period because, on top of not being able to walk or just go outside for fresh air, the local authority was already cancelling support for carers coming into homes for fear of contracting the virus. Physiotherapists cancelled sessions. They believed that I was one of the younger survivors, and therefore there was fear that, because of visiting elderly patients, they could bring the virus to me. So, literally, I was left to fend for myself. Additionally, people who used to come and visit and do my shopping couldn't do that. They would call and leave food at my doorstep. There was a week when I didn't see a person. I would just see people passing by. You could sense that people were scared because

Covid had just hit the whole world. It was a very lonely place. I could have had mental health issues, but God preserved me. I had to feed my soul and spirit with the Word, watching the Gospel channels, listening to worship music and live streaming services from church. The services kept me going and gave me hope and something to look forward to. I remember a worship session with a specific guest worship leader who shared a testimony similar to mine and how God had healed him. His powerful testimony just bolstered my faith.

It feels as if the Lord allowed me to face adversity in a foreign land so that I might experience His goodness – and I know what it means when He says in His Word: "Taste and see that the Lord is good." I have tasted His goodness. I might have taken his divine providence for granted if I were among my people. The other lesson I learned throughout this journey is that the church became practical – for me, the church is not a building or a gathering. I experienced so much love and kindness from the body of Christ. Some of my brothers and sisters in Christ were so intentional in the manner in which they cared for me. They loved me to health; they had servants' hearts. I have seen people going out of their way to support me and hold my hand. When the Bible talks about being each other's keepers, I have witnessed that – the church became my strength and my rock, especially during the months of lockdown. I knew that there would be either a phone call, a knock at the door, someone coming to pray for me or bringing me food. Or just coming round to have fellowship and spend time with me or provide for my grooming and physical needs.

It was just so palpable and touching to see the body of Christ rally around one of their own and give so much of their time. It wasn't only about financial support – people were giving their time.

It also felt as if God was slowing me down and teaching me to depend on Him because I felt that I was doing good at some point but was not doing God. My work was becoming an idol. I would miss out on worship rehearsals or be late to prayers at church because of work. I was self-reliant, but God had to take away my mere salary so that I could learn to depend on Him and Him alone.

I know that the Lord preserved me. I have put this book together to demonstrate that we overcome by the Blood of the Lamb and the Word of our testimony. This illness would have taken me out, if God had not covered and protected me. I am still making strides on this journey; the joy of the Lord is my strength. Sometimes I just stand in awe of His healing grace, from carrying a lifeless left side of your body to being able to get on public transport on your own. How I recovered from being hoisted onto the toilet to being able to undertake my self-care independently. It's so surreal when I think about the moments of relying on a Sara Stedy for bathroom trips to being able to get in the shower independently without support.

Truthvine Church and certain individuals in the body of Christ that Father God has assigned to me made me realise what it means to be part of the body and how the body can work together. Especially when one of their own is going through an affliction – experiencing a period of adversity. All those God assigned to me showered me with so much love, the love of Jesus. And I wouldn't have come so far in this journey if it was not for their godly support.

Sometimes, I pondered whether the Lord allowed this to happen so that He could heal my body, soul and spirit. It felt like the Lord wanted to heal me from childhood wounds when I had to re-learn how to master fine motor skills (tying shoelaces, fastening and unbuttoning clothes, cutting vegetables, et cetera) and gross motor skills (walking, standing, lifting, et cetera). I have learned to appreciate even small things in life, and to be thankful to the Lord for life. You appreciate every little milestone that you make, like being able to fasten hooks, wear earrings, and climb the stairs – they bring such an amazing sense of achievement

I am still on my healing journey, but you know what? – I feel I have overcome!

Because the Sovereign Lord helps me, I will not be disgraced. Therefore, have I set my face like flint, and I know I will not be put to shame. (Isaiah 50:7)

About the Author

Where do you start describing Zola or her character? Let me start by saying she is such a warm person.

Her warmth dominates her whole character. She is a friend from whom you would not want to part. She has a way of making everyone feel important by the way she intently listens, and her expressions radiate from her face to her whole being. She does not speak without understanding, and her advice is salient and timely, and always filled with consideration.

Zola is dependable, trustworthy and always keeps her promises. She is always there when you need her, to listen and to support wherever she can. Zola is a peacemaker who is pained when there is conflict and can always bring out the best in situations.

She is a family-orientated person, and her immediate and extended family reciprocate her love for them. She enjoys telling stories and can captivate her audience.

Zola was born in South Africa in a small township called Ginsberg where she grew up and was educated. She moved to Alice and studied at the University of Fort Hare, where she read Social Work.

Zola worked as a social worker in South Africa before emigrating to England to work as a social worker, until her work was interrupted by what she calls a Monster Attack.

Website:
www.zolamangcotywa.co.uk

Instagram:
https://www.instagram/zolamangcotywa

Facebook:
https://www.facebook.com/nokuzola.mangcotywa/

Useful Agency

The Stroke Association

Stroke Helpline open:

Telephone: 0303 3033 100

https://www.stroke.org.uk/finding-support/support-services

References

Thompson, Phil and Zenzo Matoga (2018) "My Worship" lyrics © Integrity Worship Music, Zenzo Matoga Music,

@philthompsonworship

Printed in Great Britain
by Amazon